W9-BAU-543

IV
XC
LDM

THE STORY OF NUMBERS

Long ago, people had no numbers. How did they discover the idea of numbers? How did they learn to count? What were the first written numbers like?

This book explains early number systems—and shows why the numbers we use today are the best the world has ever known.

This new edition of THE STORY OF NUMBERS has been thoroughly revised and updated to conform with New Math vocabulary and concept.

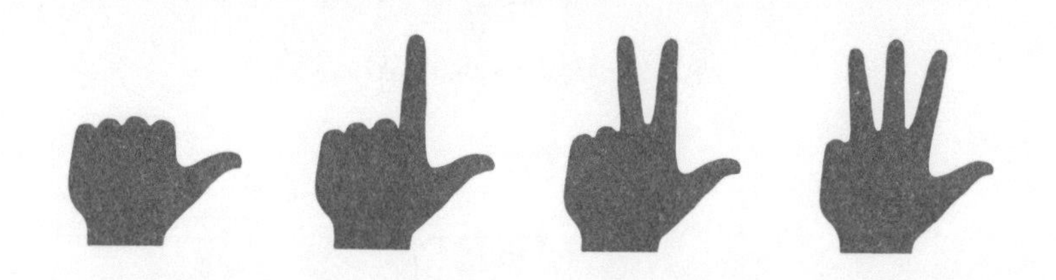

MCMLXVI

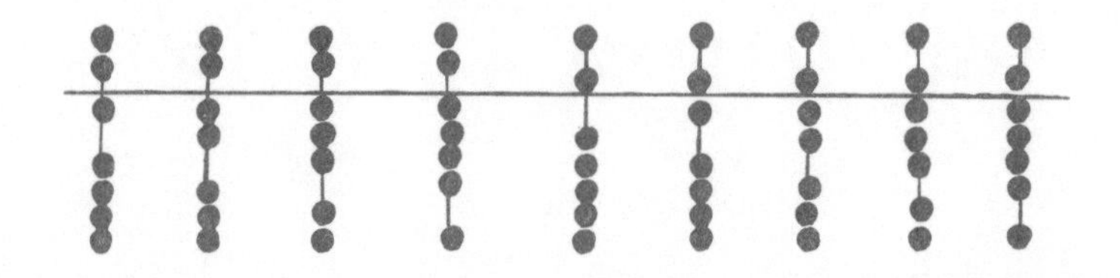

0 1 2 3 4 5 6 7 8 9

THE STORY OF NUMBERS

PATRICIA LAUBER

illustrated by Mircea Vasiliu

RANDOM HOUSE • NEW YORK

We would like to thank Professor Ernest E. Allen
of Southern Colorado State College
for his thorough reading of, and his most helpful comments on,
this new edition of THE STORY OF NUMBERS.

Fifth Printing, 1966

Library of Congress Catalog Card Number: 61-7769

Manufactured in the United States of America

Design: Patricia de Groot

Contents

THE STORY OF NUMBERS

1

World of Numbers

You live in a world of numbers. From the time you get up till the time you go to bed, your whole day is full of numbers. Perhaps you:

Get up when the alarm rings at 7 o'clock.

Walk 9 blocks to school.

Have 5 classes and get a 90 in arithmetic.

Lose 4 marbles through a hole in your pocket.

Find 10¢ on the sidewalk.

The sizes of your clothes are numbers. You use numbers to telephone. The numbers on a calendar help you keep track of days and months. The page numbers in this book help you find your place.

Your food is measured and weighed in numbers. The price of a movie ticket is a number. So is the score of a baseball game.

Everything around you was made with the help of numbers. Men use numbers to build:

Bridges, roads, houses.

Automobiles, airplanes, ships, trains, bicycles.

TV and radio sets.

Tables, chairs, desks, beds.

They use numbers to make clocks, ladders, pencils, books, rugs, footballs, dolls, and cakes.

You work with numbers, too. You are always using them to answer questions like: How far? How many? How heavy? How much? How often? How soon?

In our modern world, numbers are everyday things. We learn about them when we are very young. We use them all the time. We really

2ND ST.
13-61
34
TO CENTER 1mi
25 MPH
4 eggs
2 cups flour
1/2 cup s.
MARCH
S M T W T F S
1 2 3 4
5 6 7 8 9 10 11
12 13 14 15 16 17 18
19 20 21 22 23 24 25
26 27 28 29 30 31
5 lbs.
MILK
1 Qt.
1 lb

could not get on without them. In fact, it is hard to imagine a world without numbers.

Yet, at one time, there was such a world. For numbers have not always been everyday things.

A few thousand years ago, only wise men could do arithmetic. Still earlier, no one knew how to add or multiply. Before that, most people couldn't count. Earlier still, there simply were no numbers. Men had not discovered them.

The discovery of numbers was slow and hard. It took men thousands of years to discover what you have learned in just a few years.

Why did it take so long? To understand, you must forget everything you know about numbers. You must even forget that there are such things.

2

One, Two, Three, Many

Suppose you live in a distant forest. You are alone. There is no one to teach you anything. You learn only by seeing, doing, and remembering.

Every morning the sun rises. You've learned where to look for it. You've learned that the sun brings light and heat.

You hear the song of a brook and you know it means water.

You see berries, shining with dew. Because they are blue-black, you know they are ripe for eating.

You see marks on soft earth. They tell you a rabbit has hopped this way.

The sun sinks low and you know darkness is near. Soon the moon and stars will fill the sky.

You know all this and much more. But you know nothing about numbers, for there are none to be seen. The sharpest eyes will never spy a 1 striding along a trail. They'll never see a 2 swinging from a tree. They'll never find a fat 3 curled up under a bush.

Numbers are not things that anyone can see, like trees or rocks. Numbers are ideas. They do not live in forests. They live in the mind.

Would you ever think of numbers? Would you ever discover them?

It doesn't seem very likely.

Living simply in your forest, you wouldn't really need numbers.

For instance, you wouldn't need to know that you had picked *six* handfuls of berries. You would need to know something else. Had you picked *enough* berries for your supper? You could tell that just by looking at them.

So, you wouldn't need to count. And if you didn't need to, you wouldn't discover numbers.

That was why very early peoples did not discover numbers. They lived so simply that they didn't need numbers. They lived so simply that they didn't even need many words for talking.

The first people who even came close to numbers lived about 25,000 years ago.

These people were wanderers, who had no towns or villages. They roamed from place to place, seeking food. They hunted animals and birds. They gathered berries, nuts, roots, and grain. Their clothes were animal skins. They made their few weapons and tools from stone. That is why we call them Stone Age people.

In the Stone Age, men knew nothing of numbers. They could not count, and they didn't need to. They needed only to know whether they had enough. Had they gathered enough berries? Enough nuts? Enough grain? Did they have enough fuel for a fire? They learned to tell by looking.

But their eyes also told them something else. And this thing pushed them close to counting.

They saw that  was different from  . And they saw that  were not the same as  .

Or suppose a man went hunting with . When he returned, he had . He knew that was different from the he had gone out with.

Now, it was fine to see that  and  and  were all different. But people needed a way of saying so.

A man came home from hunting. He wanted to tell his friends that he had caught  — not  or  . How could he do this?

In time, people found a way. They made up some new words.

Probably they had a word for  .

They made up a word for  .

They made up another word for  .

But the words were not real number words. The word for [deer] [deer] meant only [deer] [deer]. It could not be used to talk about [tree] [tree] or [spear] [spear] or [person] [person] or anything else. To talk about those, people used different sets of words.

Suppose we still talked that way today. Then for deer we might say:

deer

badeer

fadeer

But for spears we might say:

spear

ugspear

mugspear

For pebbles we would have still another set of words. And we would have still more sets of words for people, days, caves, rivers, hills, and so on.

But, luckily, we don't talk that way. At some time long ago, our ancestors took a huge leap forward. They discovered the idea of numbers.

They looked at 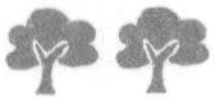 and  and  .
They saw that all these things were very different. Yet in one way the things were alike. They were alike in number. One word could be used to say that number. The same word could be used with trees, deer, pebbles, and everything else.

Used with trees, it would mean 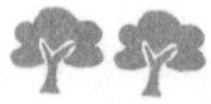 .

Used with deer, it would mean  .

Used with pebbles, it would mean .

We don't know how men discovered the idea of two. But somehow they did. They had never seen a two anywhere. Still, they learned that there was such a thing as two.

After two, it was easy to discover three.

But three was as far as people went. More than three was simply "many" or "a pile" or "a lot." No one knew about four or five or any other number.

If that seems strange, remember that these people knew chiefly what their eyes told them.

They saw that ● ● were different from ● ● ●.
But these pebbles ● ● ● ● ● ● looked just like these pebbles ● ● ● ● ● ● ●. Unless you count, they will look the same to you. So ● ● ● ● ● ● like ● ● ● ● ● ● ● was "many."

With the discovery of one, two, and three, men took a great step forward. Numbers became a new weapon for them. It was the most powerful weapon they owned.

With spears they could hunt. With axes they could defend themselves. But with numbers they began to master the world around them. They did so even when they could not count beyond three.

One, two, three, many. That is the way most people still see today. You do, too. To prove it, first read these rules. Then try the test at the end of this chapter.

The test is made up of six lines of drawings. You start by covering up all the drawings with a sheet of paper.

Pull the sheet down until you can see the first row. Glance at the row and look away. How many apples did you see?

Pull the paper down a little more. Glance at the second row. Look away. How many birds did you see?

Do the same thing with each of the rows.

The hardest part of the test is to keep yourself from counting. Try very hard not to count. Just take a quick look at each line of drawings.

You will find that it is easy to see three. Perhaps you will be able to see four. But after that you cannot tell how many you see unless you count.

Try giving this test to other people. You will find they can't do any better than you can.

The test shows you why early peoples stopped counting at three. Five looked just like six to them. Eight looked like nine.

Now, get a sheet of paper. Then turn the page and take the test.

A 

B 

C

D

E

F

3

Seasons and Sheep

People could count to three. But they were still wanderers, who roamed about seeking food. Whenever they found a good place, they camped there for a few months. Then they packed up and moved on. Behind them they left their rubbish—bones, old tools and weapons, grain scattered on the ground.

Sometimes a tribe found a place it liked very much. It went back to this place the next year. Going back, the people noticed something. On the ground of their old camp, grain plants were growing. In time the people learned where these plants came from. The plants had grown from grain left on the ground.

That gave the people an idea. They learned to set aside some grain for planting each year. Doing so, they became farmers. That was about 8,000 years ago.

Around the same time, people discovered something else. They could herd animals, keeping them in groups. This was much easier than going hunting for meat. And so they became shepherds and herders.

People began to settle in villages. They no

longer had to search for food. They could raise their own.

This new life brought a great need for counting.

Farmers had to keep track of the seasons. When was it time to sow? When was it time to harvest? When would the calves be born? Farmers could not answer these questions by counting, "One, two, three, many."

Shepherds had to keep track of their flocks. Did they have all their sheep? Were some lost? Had new lambs been born? "One, two, three, many" did not help the shepherds either.

How could farmers keep track of the seasons? How could shepherds keep track of their flocks?

Men found a way. They invented the tally.

A tally is a simple kind of record. The record is made up of a series of marks. Each mark stands for one thing.

Probably you have often made a tally. Suppose you're playing tick-tack-toe. How do you keep

your score? You put down one mark for each game you win. When you have won three games, your tally looks like this: ///. For four games, your tally shows: ////. After four, it is hard to see just how many marks you have. So for the fifth game you do this: ~~////~~.

When you keep track of games that way, you are tallying. And your tally is much like the tallies used by farmers and shepherds of long ago.

Farmers tallied the passing of time by cutting notches in wood. For each day, a farmer cut a new notch. Each time the moon came full, he cut a special notch—perhaps a big one. By the end of a year, he had a rough calendar. During the next year, he used this calendar to keep track of how time was passing.

Shepherds used tallies to keep track of their sheep.

Some shepherds cut notches in wood. They cut one notch for each sheep.

Other shepherds tallied with pebbles. For each sheep, they placed one pebble in their pile.

A tally gave the shepherd a record of his sheep. He could match sheep with notches or pebbles. Then he could tell if any of the sheep were lost.

Tallies were very useful. By tallying, people could answer many questions. They could tell "How soon?" or "Are they all here?" or "Is there enough?"

But there was one question a tally could not answer. That was the important question "How many?"

Suppose a shepherd tallied his flock of sheep. At the end, he still did not know how many sheep he had. He just had a stick with a lot of notches on it. Or perhaps he had a large pile of pebbles.

Was his flock bigger than his neighbor's? Finding out was a long job. The two shepherds had to sit down with their tallies. Then they matched notch for notch or pebble for pebble.

Was this year's flock bigger than last year's? If the shepherd had last year's tally, he could work out the answer. If he had lost the tally, he could not tell.

What people needed was a better way of tallying. They needed a way that would help them remember.

In time, people found that way. They began to tally on their fingers.

4

Fingers and Toes

Fingers were the best tallies in the world. The reason was a simple one. Fingers were attached to the hands.

That probably sounds like a strange reason. But imagine that you are a shepherd, thousands of years ago. You want to tally the baby lambs in your flock.

You pick up a good stick. You reach for your knife. And you find you've forgotten it. Your knife is back in the village.

You decide to use pebbles instead. You tally the lambs with pebbles. Then you trip and drop the pebbles. Your morning's work is lost. You must start all over again. For you cannot count in numbers. You do not know how many pebbles you had.

If you are tallying on your fingers, neither of these accidents can happen.

You can't forget your fingers. They are always with you.

Nor can you drop your fingers. They are attached to your hands. They cannot fall out of your pocket and get mixed up with a lot of other fingers.

But there is something else even better about fingers: they are always in the same order. Your thumb is always in the same place. So are the rest of your fingers. You know just how your fingers look on your hands. And that makes fingers much better than pebbles for tallying. Fingers form a pattern that is easy to remember.

Suppose you tally your young lambs with pebbles. The pebbles look like this: ● ● ● ● ● ● ●

That doesn't tell you very much. You know

only that you have "many" pebbles. There is no way you can remember ●●●●●●● .

Now suppose you make the same tally, using your fingers. You put up one finger for each lamb. When you finish, you have:

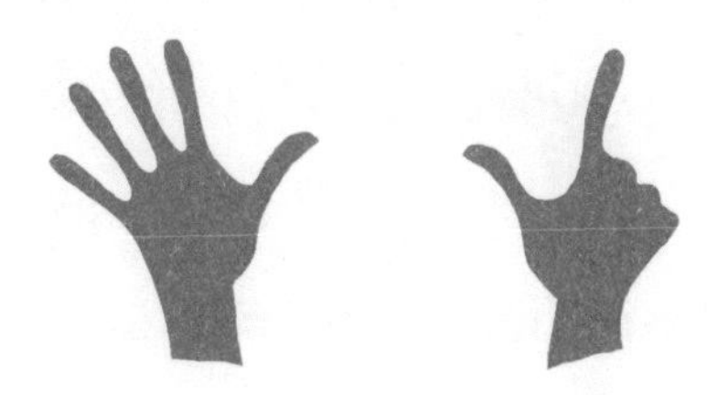

That makes a picture in your mind. It is easy to remember. And later it is easy to check the lambs against the picture.

Or perhaps you think of a still better way of remembering your finger tally. You give it a name. The name is "all the fingers on one hand and two on the other."

And that is what shepherds thought of doing, about 7,000 years ago. Finger tallying led them into using number names.

They already had words for one, two, three, and many. Some people also had a word for four. Finger tallying soon gave them a word for five. It was the same word they used for "hand."

Once started, people easily learned to count to ten. Here is the way their number words went, after four:

hand (5)
one on the other hand (6)
two on the other hand (7)
three on the other hand (8)
four on the other hand (9)
both hands (10).

In some parts of the world, people used their toes as well as their fingers. They counted through ten on their fingers. Starting with eleven, they counted on their toes. After ten, their number words went something like this:

one on the foot (11)
two on the foot (12)

three on the foot (13)
four on the foot (14)
whole foot (15)
one on the other foot (16)
two on the other foot (17)
three on the other foot (18)
four on the other foot (19)
both feet (20).

Such number names can be very clumsy. We know this because some have turned up in far-away corners of the world. For instance, not long ago, a tribe of Indians in South America still counted on fingers and toes. Their word for ten was *lanàmrihegem.* It meant "the fingers of both hands." That wasn't too bad a word. But for twenty, the Indians said "the fingers of both hands and both feet." In their language this came out *lanàmrihegem cat gracherhaka anamichirihegem!*

Perhaps the very early number names were not quite that bad. But they were long and clumsy. So in time they changed. They became shorter. People no longer said "three on the other hand" if they meant eight. They used a shorter word that meant eight and only eight.

These short words were the first true number names.

Tallying on fingers was a big step forward in the story of numbers. Fingers were good because they were attached to the hands. Better yet, they led to number names. With names, people learned to count higher. With names, people could talk about numbers. Other people understood what they meant. And that was very important.

One other thing about fingers was even more important. There were only ten of them. And that made counting easier yet.

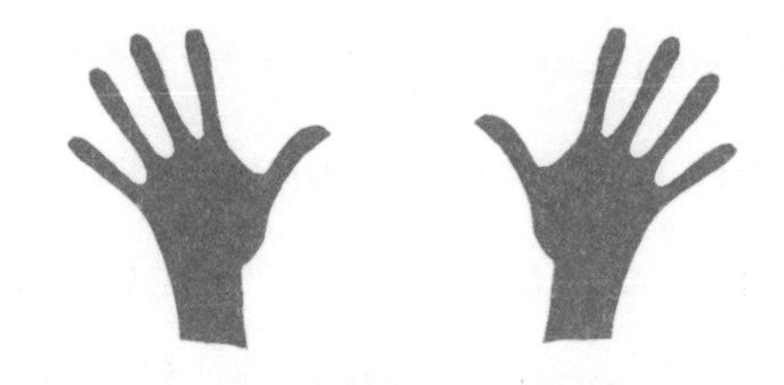

5

Ten and Begin Again

You are counting on your fingers. You reach ten—and you run out of fingers.

At first that doesn't seem to be much of a help. Wouldn't counting be easier if you had more fingers? Suppose you had thirty fingers. Then you could count up to thirty without stopping. Or suppose you had fifty fingers. Wouldn't that be even better?

The answer is no. More fingers would make counting harder.

With lots of fingers, you would be like the shepherd making notches on a stick. If he cut twenty notches, they didn't mean much. He saw only a lot of notches.

When the shepherd counted on his fingers, that was different. He counted up to ten and ran out of fingers. So he began again and counted up to ten a second time. Then he knew that he had twice used up all his fingers. The number of his sheep was "both hands twice."

Fingers put a pattern into counting. On fingers, people had to count in groups of ten. That pattern made it easy to keep track of the numbers. They counted up to ten. They began again and counted up to ten. That gave them two-tens. Then they came to three-tens, four-tens, five-tens, and so on.

We count in much the same way today.

Without a pattern, counting would be much

harder. Try making up a set of number words for one to a hundred. You can easily find a hundred different words. But how are you going to remember a hundred number words and what they mean? How can you remember the order they come in? The easiest way is to have a pattern for your words.

That was what early people did. They didn't choose a pattern. Probably they didn't even know that a pattern made counting easier. But fingers gave them a pattern. They counted in groups of ten—or sometimes groups of five. People who also used their toes counted in groups of twenty.

A tribe in Africa today counts in fives. Their counting goes something like this:

1 - wean	6 - judom wean (5 and 1)
2 - yar	7 - judom yar (5 and 2)
3 - yat	8 - judom yat (5 and 3)
4 - yanet	9 - judom yanet (5 and 4)
5 - judom	10 - rook.

Here is the way some English shepherds used

to count. Look carefully at the words. You will see how the shepherds made up words for numbers after ten. You will also see something that helped them remember the number words. Pairs of words rhyme. There are two pairs of rhyming words. Then there is one very different word. It marks a five. And five was the end of the fingers on one hand.

1 - yan	11 - yanadick
2 - tyan	12 - tyanadick
3 - tethera	13 - tetheradick
4 - methera	14 - metheradick
5 - *jimp*	15 - *bumfit*
6 - sethera	16 - yanabumfit
7 - lethera	17 - tyanabumfit
8 - hovera	18 - tetherabumfit
9 - dovera	19 - metherabumfit
10 - *dick*	20 - *jiggit*.

The Mayas of Central America were a people who counted with a pattern of twenty. So did the Aztecs.

So did the ancestors of today's French people. Some French number words show this very clearly. For example, the French word for 80 means four-twenties.

Five, ten, twenty—the number doesn't matter. The important thing is the pattern. With a pattern, people can count higher and higher. They can count as high as they need to. And they can easily keep track of where they are.

Early peoples probably did not count much higher than a thousand. They didn't have to. They didn't have that many sheep or eggs or anything else. Really big numbers came much later in man's history.

Long before that, men took the next step forward. They learned to write numbers. Written numbers are called "numerals." They may also be called "number signs" or "number symbols."

6

∩∩∩∩∩ ||| and 五十三

Farmers, you remember, were the first makers of calendars. By tallying, they could make a rough calendar. This calendar showed a year as being 360 days long.

But a year is not 360 days long. It is 365¼ days long. So the first calendars did not work very well. Each year was wrong by 5¼ days. After six years, the calendar was wrong by a month. That made problems for the farmers.

The wise men of the villages began to work on new calendars. They studied the sun. They noted how its position in the sky changed from season to season. They studied the stars. They saw that many stars also change their position in the sky.

Some even vanish at certain times of year.

With long study, wise men measured the passing of time. Over hundreds of years, they came closer and closer to measuring the true length of a year.

These wise men had to remember many things. They had to remember where the sun was each day. They had to remember what stars shone each night. And they had to remember these facts over long periods of time.

So the wise men kept written records. Among the things they had to write down were numbers. Out of calendar-making came the first written numbers.

There were early calendar-makers in several parts of the world. None knew about the other calendar-makers. Each group invented its own way of writing numerals. It made little signs that stood for numbers.

The rest of this chapter shows you some of the early number signs, or numerals.

EGYPT

Some of the first written numbers were used in Egypt about 5,000 years ago. Egyptian numerals began as notches in wood or stone. These were used to record passing days. Then the Egyptians learned to write on papyrus. Papyrus was made from strips of reeds pressed together. The Egyptians wrote on it with a brush. Using a brush, they could make many different shapes for numbers.

MESOPOTAMIA

The people of a second land also invented numerals about 5,000 years ago. This land was Mesopotamia. It, too, was near the Mediterranean Sea. But it was many miles away from Egypt. Its people had no way of knowing what the Egyptians were doing. But they made the same kind of invention.

Here, though, the signs were a very different shape. The reason was this. In Mesopotamia people wrote on soft clay with a pointed stick. The stick made marks the shape of a wedge.

The people who invented these numerals were called Sumerians. Their numerals were also used by later peoples who came to live in Mesopotamia, such as the Babylonians.

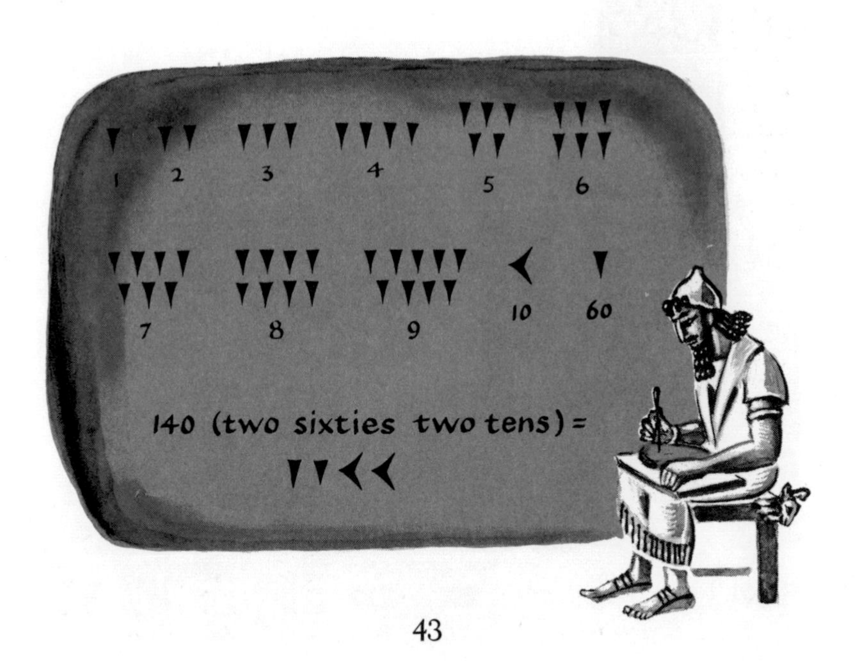

CENTRAL AMERICA

The Mayas of Central America were also farmers, builders, makers of calendars, and inventors of number signs.

The Mayas counted on their fingers and their toes. So they used a pattern of twenty in their number signs. In writing small numbers, they used two signs—dots for ones and lines for fives.

Using dots and lines, they could write any number up to nineteen:

For some bigger numbers they used an oval. When they put an oval under another symbol, they made it twenty times bigger: = 20 = 40 = 60

A number such as forty-five was written as two twenties and one five: Notice the spacing. It tells you the symbol is for forty-five and not for seven.

CHINA

The Chinese also invented numerals very early. Their signs for one, two, and three come from tallying. After that the Chinese made up signs. They invented signs for 4, 5, 6, 7, 8, 9, 10, 100, 1,000, and 10,000. With those signs they could write any number.

The examples show you how they did it.

12 is made up of 10 and 2. It is 10 + 2. So they wrote the sign for 2 *under* the sign for 10. That meant the two numbers were added.

20 is also made up of 10 and 2. But it is 10 × 2. So they wrote the sign for 2 *above* the 10. That showed the two numbers were multiplied.

Other numbers were made by both adding and multiplying. Look at the sign for 52. It says 10 × 5 + 2.

7

Letters for Numbers

In early times, people wrote by drawing tiny pictures. Each picture stood for a word or an idea.

The pictures made both writing and reading hard. The man who was writing had to know thousands of little signs. So did the man who was reading.

Then, about 3,000 years ago, the first alphabet was invented. With an alphabet, people used letters to make words, just as we do. The alphabet made reading and writing much easier.

And that gave certain people an idea.

"The alphabet makes it easy to write words," they said. "Perhaps the alphabet would also make it easy to write numbers." They decided to try.

They gave up using little drawings for numbers. They used letters instead.

One people who did this were the Greeks.

The Romans also used letters for numbers.

The Romans wrote their smallest numbers with strokes: I, II, III. For 5 they used V. 10 was X. 50 was L.

For bigger numbers, they used the first letter of the number word. *Centum* was their word for hundred. So they wrote C for 100. *Mille* meant thousand. So M stood for 1,000.

Roman number signs were neat, clear, and easy to write. But, like other old number signs, they were clumsy to work with. They were all clumsy for the same reason.

Every number sign had to do two jobs. It had to be a number. And it had to tell what kind of number this was—a ten, a hundred, or a thousand. That is, the number sign also had to be a label.

ROME

The Romans used letters for their numbers. We still use the Roman numerals on some of our books and clocks and buildings.

To see how that worked, look first at our own number signs.

For five, we use this sign: 5

We use the same sign to write fifty. But we move the sign one place to the left: 50

For five hundred, we move it two places to the left: 500

For five thousand, we move it over three places: 5,000

So we do not need labels. The place tells us what kind of number our five is being used for.

But Roman number signs did not work that way.

For five, a Roman used this sign: V

But for fifty he did not move it over one place. He used a different sign: L

For five hundred, he used a third sign: D

For five thousand, he used five of his thousand signs: MMMMM

For us, place shows the difference between 5 and 50.

For the Romans, the number sign had to be a label. V was five, and L was fifty.

This meant that the Romans had to have many number signs, not just a few.

It also meant that Roman number signs often took up a lot of space.

For example, suppose we want to write down this number: four thousand four hundred fifty-eight.

Here it is in our numerals: 4,458.

Here it is in Roman numerals:

MMMMCCCCLVIII.

Such numerals made arithmetic very hard.

Imagine having to multiply

MMMCCXXXVII by CCLXXV

Or what if you had to divide

MMMMCCCCXLIV by CXI

Just thinking about it is enough to make your head ache.

And the number signs of Egypt and Mesopotamia were every bit as bad as Roman ones.

Perhaps you wonder how the ancients managed to do arithmetic at all.

Well, many people didn't need to do any.

Others learned to do simple arithmetic on their fingers. Suppose a man wanted to add three and four. He put up three fingers. Then he put up four more. Counting his fingers, he found that three and four make seven.

But early wise men had to solve much harder problems. They had to work with bigger numbers. So they invented a way of doing arithmetic without using number signs. They did their arithmetic on an abacus, which is also called a counting board.

At the end of this book, you can find out how an abacus works.

At first only wise men did hard arithmetic. But, as time went by, other people had to learn to work with numbers. For instance, merchants had to add and subtract.

By Roman times, many people knew some

MMMCCXXXVII
CCLXXV

arithmetic. Boys learned it in school. But they were taught only simple arithmetic—the kind they could do on their fingers. Really hard arithmetic was done by slaves on the abacus.

Roman number signs were clumsy. They were not made for doing arithmetic. Yet they were used for a long time by many people. They were used for hundreds of years after Rome ceased to be a great nation.

Sometimes they are still used today. You see them on the faces of some clocks. You find them in the front of some books. You see them on the cornerstones of some buildings.

But, luckily, we do not use Roman number signs much. We work with very different signs. These came to us from India.

8

Nothing and New Numerals

Long before the time of Rome, a great people lived in India. They were the Hindus.

The Hindus knew nothing about Egypt or Mesopotamia. They knew nothing about China. But they made the same discoveries men had made in those lands. They were farmers. They were calendar-makers. They were builders. And they were inventors. They invented a way to write words. They invented a way to write numerals.

Their first number signs were just strokes—the same strokes they used in tallying.

Then the Hindus learned to write on dried palm leaves. Their writing became more flowing. And they began to join up the strokes of their number signs. = became २. And ≡ became ३. After a while, the Hindus had nine such number signs.

This is the way Hindu number signs looked about a thousand years ago:

१ २ ३ ४ ५ ६ ७ ८ ९

1 2 3 4 5 6 7 8 9

These number signs were good. They were quick and easy to write. They took up little room.

The way the Hindus used their signs was also good. With just nine signs, they could write any number. For example, five thousand five hundred fifty-five was ५५५५.

This made Hindu number signs very easy to work with. Number signs stood for numbers. They did not have to be labels as well. The place of a numeral told how it was being used. २४२ clearly meant two hundred forty-two.

There was just one problem.

Suppose a man wanted to write two hundred

two. He wrote it this way: २ २, leaving a space between the two number signs. The space was supposed to show that the number was two hundred two.

But that was not very clear. Someone else could easily mistake the number. He might read it as twenty-two or as two thousand two.

The problem bothered Hindus who worked with numbers. Finally, someone thought of a way to solve it. Whenever he had an empty space between two number signs, he put a small mark in it. If he had two empty spaces, he used two marks. Then it was easy to tell २·२ from २२ or २··२.

This mark began as a small dot. Later it changed to a small circle—the circle we call zero.

The Hindu zero was a truly great invention.

No other ancient people had a zero. To them, nothing was—well, nothing. You didn't make a mark to stand for nothing. Marks meant *some* thing—two sheep, five bowls, four girls.

But the Hindus saw they could use a mark to mean nothing. They saw that this mark would be very useful.

And so it was. It gave the Hindus the best set of number signs in the world. With only ten signs, a man could express any number. The numerals were small, neat, and easy to work with.

Fortunately, the Hindus were traders. Traveling, they carried with them both goods and ideas. They took their new numerals to the city of Baghdad about 1,200 years ago.

From Baghdad, the numerals were taken westward by the Arabs of North Africa. In time, Arab numerals spread to Spain. From Spain, the number signs traveled to the rest of Europe.

The shape of the number signs changed many times during those travels. They changed as different men wrote them.

Then, about 600 years ago, printing was invented. Number signs took a shape and kept it. They were much like the numerals we use today.

ATLANTIC OCEAN
EUROPE
FRANCE
SPAIN
ITALY
GREEC
MEDITERRANEAN
N
W
E
S
NORTH AFRICA

Our numerals started in India. Hindu traders carried them west to the great city of Baghdad. From there, Arabs took the numerals to North Africa and Europe.

9

Number Names

Perhaps you wonder why only the Hindus had really good number signs. Why didn't other peoples think of them, too? The easiest way to explain it is this:

Suppose you climb a huge hill that is covered with trees and rocks. As you climb, you take the way that seems best. At the top of the hill, you look back down. From there you see that you did not take the easiest way. There is a better way than the one you followed. But you can't see it until you reach the top.

Ancient peoples were climbing a hill of numerals.

Today we stand at the top of this hill.

0 1 2 3 4 5 6 7 8 9
X M C
九 十

THE PATTERN OF OUR NUMBER SIGNS

Read down the left-hand row. It shows our ten number signs. With them we write all other numbers, big and small. Do you see the pattern in the way the bigger number signs are written?

0	10	20	30	40	50	60	70	80	90	100
1	11	21	31	41	51	61	71	81	91	101
2	12	22	32	42	52	62	72	82	92	102
3	13	23	33	43	53	63	73	83	93	103
4	14	24	34	44	54	64	74	84	94	104
5	15	25	35	45	55	65	75	85	95	105
6	16	26	36	46	56	66	76	86	96	106
7	17	27	37	47	57	67	77	87	97	107
8	18	28	38	48	58	68	78	88	98	108
9	19	29	39	49	59	69	79	89	99	109

Looking back, we see that the Hindu path was the best.

From the top of the hill, we also see that our numerals are very fine indeed.

We have only ten number signs—0, 1, 2, 3, 4, 5, 6, 7, 8, 9. With them we can write any number at all. Small numbers are written with them. So are big numbers.

The pattern of our number signs is very clear. You cannot get lost among the numbers. You always know what comes next.

Our number names are almost as simple as our number signs. After twelve, they form an easy-to-remember pattern.

Our oldest number names are one, two, three, four, five, six, seven, eight, nine, ten. These words are so old that no one knows where they came from. No one knows what they first meant. But there is one clue that takes us back to fingers.

We have a name for all single numbers—0, 1,

2, 3, 4, 5, 6, 7, 8, 9. We call them digits. 2 is a digit. So is 7. Any single number is a digit. And digit has still another meaning in English. It means "finger" or "toe."

So we can guess that our very old number names were once finger words.

The next two number words are eleven and twelve. They are also very old. But we do know something about them.

Eleven used to mean "one left over."

Twelve used to mean "two left over."

The two words go back to the time when people counted on their fingers. Say that a woman was counting eggs. She counted up to ten on her fingers. She found she had that many eggs—and one more. So the number of her eggs was "one left over." Or perhaps she had two left over—twelve.

In time the "left-overs" became number names. One-left-over was the name for the number that followed ten. Two-left-over was the

name for the next number.

After twelve the pattern starts.

Thirteen was once "three-and-ten." It was three fingers after ten. But people ran their words together when they spoke of this number. And so "three-and-ten" turned into thirteen.

Fourteen is closer to its parent words. It was once "four-and-ten."

Fifteen was born when people ran "five-and-ten" together.

Sixteen, seventeen, eighteen, and nineteen were born in the same way.

Now you begin to see where the other number words came from.

Twenty was once "two-tens."

Thirty was "three-tens."

Forty was "four-tens."

Fifty was "five-tens."

And so it went through "nine-tens" or ninety.

All these number words come in groups of ten. You count from seven-tens through seven-tens-nine. Then you arrive at eight-tens. You count from there through eight-tens-nine. Then you arrive at nine-tens.

After nine-tens-nine comes a very different word. It is hundred. Hundred makes a good clear turning point. It shows that you have counted to ten-tens. Now it is time to begin again. You begin with one hundred. You go on to one hundred one, one hundred two, and so on.

The pattern of these number words makes them easy to remember. For they are really the same words used over and over again. And they are used over and over again in the same order. They are based on the number words for one through ten. From those ten words come all the number words from thirteen to ninety-nine.

Hundred is the first new word you come to. But with that extra word, you can count up to ten hundreds—a thousand.

Thousand makes two extra words. With two extra words, you can count way up. You go past ten thousand, past a hundred thousand. At a thousand thousand, you reach the next new word —million.

One, two, three, four, five, six, seven, eight, nine, ten, eleven, twelve, hundred, thousand.

That makes fourteen words. Put together in different ways, they take you up to 999,999, which is nine hundred ninety-nine thousand, nine hundred ninety-nine.

Hundred and thousand are both old words. No one knows where hundred came from. Probably thousand once meant "a great crowd" or "a great many." But no one is sure of that. Million, though, is a fairly new word. It is only about 600 years old. Earlier, no one needed to count that high.

The need for a bigger number arose in Italy. There were many banks. And the banks handled large sums of money. There was so much money that bankers needed a name for a thousand thousand—1,000,000.

So someone made up the name *millione*. Our word million comes from it.

At first million was only a bankers' word. To other people it meant just "a very large number." But after a while people learned that mil-

1000
1000
1.000.000

lion was not just any very big number. It was 1,000,000.

Time passed. People decided that even million wasn't a big enough number.

Around the year 1500, the French made up another new number word. It was billion. At first, billion meant million million—1,000,000,000,000. But million million turned out to be too much. People didn't need *that* big a number.

So billion came to mean only a thousand million—1,000,000,000.

Later on, someone invented trillion. It is a thousand billion—1,000,000,000,000.

Today we have names for even bigger numbers, as the table shows you. But we seldom talk of numbers bigger than a trillion. For a trillion is a very large number. A trillion seconds is 31,700 years. Traveling a trillion inches, you could:

Go around the earth 600 times and
take a round trip to the moon and
have some miles left over.

BIG NUMBERS

million	1,000,000
billion	1,000,000,000
trillion	1,000,000,000,000
quadrillion	1,000,000,000,000,000
quintillion	1,000,000,000,000,000,000
sextillion	1,000,000,000,000,000,000,000
septillion	1,000,000,000,000,000,000,000,000
octillion	1,000,000,000,000,000,000,000,000,000
nonillion	1,000,000,000,000,000,000,000,000,000,000
decillion	1,000,000,000,000,000,000,000,000,000,000,000

The next big number names are:

undecillion (36 zeros)

duodecillion (39 zeros)

tredecillion (42 zeros)

quattuordecillion (45 zeros)

quindecillion (48 zeros)

sexdecillion (51 zeros)

septendecillion (54 zeros)

octodecillion (57 zeros)

novemdecillion (60 zeros)

vigintillion (63 zeros)

Vigintillion looks like this: 1,000,000,000,000,000,000,000,-
000,000,000,000,000,000,000,000,000,000,000,000,000,000.

I II III
IV V M
X
MCX
O
1 2 3 4
5 6 7 8
9 10

Still, it doesn't matter where we stop counting. If we need to count higher, we can. The pattern is simple and clear.

Of course, the pattern isn't quite as good as it might be. If it were perfect, we would count a little differently.

We wouldn't use the words eleven and twelve at all. For they don't fit the pattern. We might change them to oneteen and twoteen. That would make them fit with thirteen, fourteen, and the other teens.

We might like to keep sixty, seventy, eighty, ninety. Those are good, clear words. But we would change twenty, thirty, forty, and fifty. We'd make them agree with the clear words. We would change them to twoty, threety, fourty, and fivety.

Or perhaps we should leave well enough alone. For, as you've seen, we have a very fine set of number signs and words. And arithmetic has never been easier.

Arithmetic Without Numerals

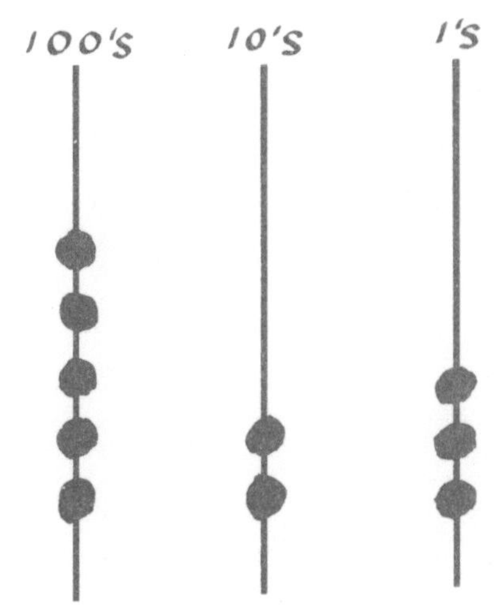

Here is an early abacus. It was made by drawing three lines in the sand. Pebbles placed on the lines stood for numbers. You can read the abacus by counting the pebbles in each line. The left-hand line tells you how many hundreds. The middle line tells you how many tens. The right-hand line tells you how many ones. The abacus is set up to show the number 523.

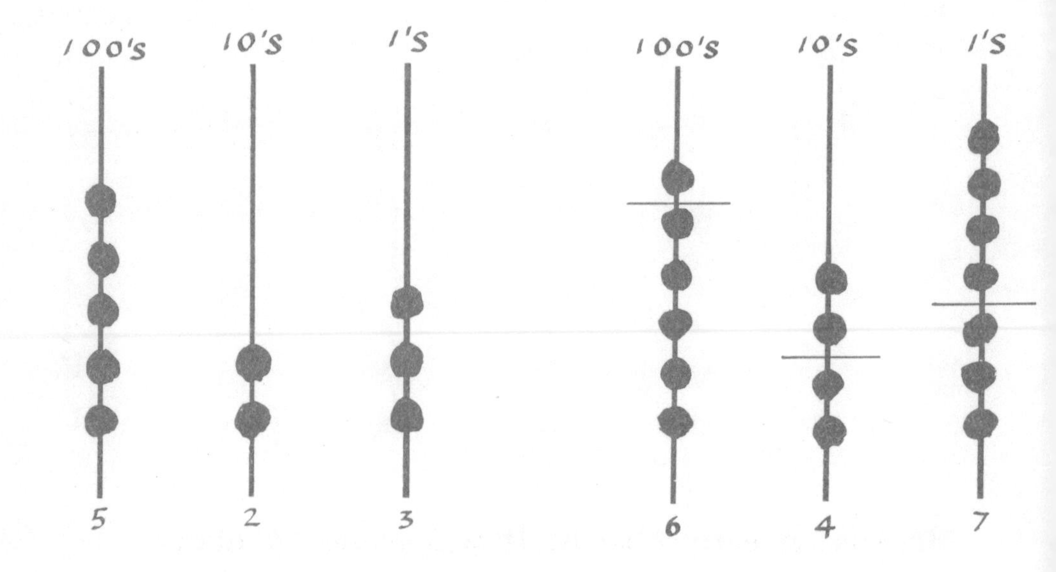

Suppose a man wanted to add 523 and 124. First he set up the number 523. Then he put 1 more pebble in the hundreds row; 2 more pebbles in the tens row; 4 more pebbles in the ones row. He counted each row of pebbles and got the answer: 647.

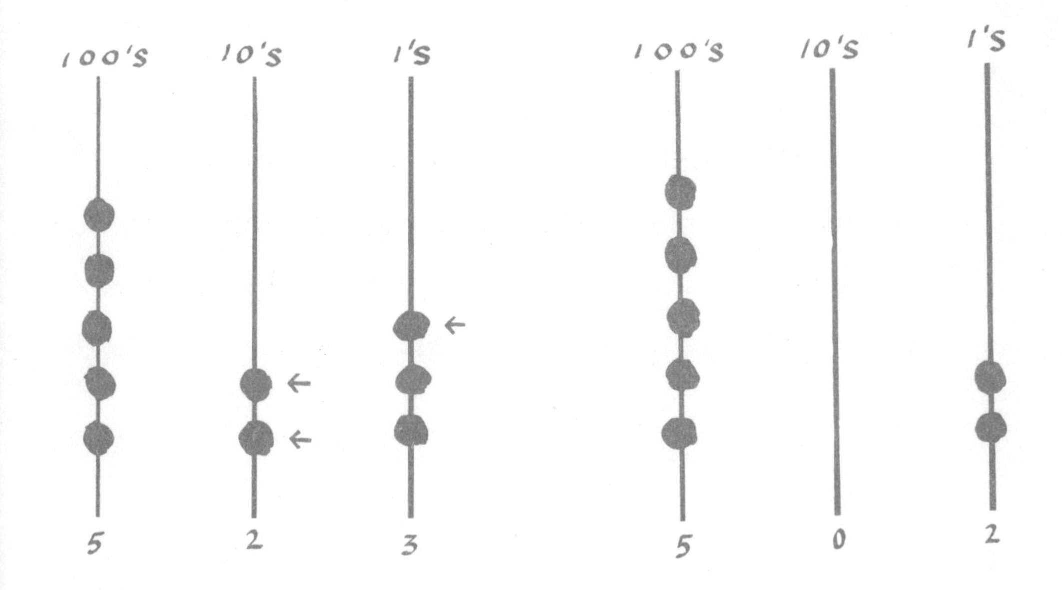

The abacus could also be used for subtracting. Suppose a man wanted to subtract 21 from 523. First he set up 523. Then he took 2 pebbles out of the tens line; he took 1 out of the ones line. He counted the remaining pebbles and got the answer: 502.

In those days people did not multiply as we do. They added. Multiplying whole numbers is really just a short way of adding. For example,

$$\begin{array}{r} 21 \\ \times 3 \\ \hline 63 \end{array} \quad \text{is another way of saying} \quad \begin{array}{r} 21 \\ 21 \\ +21 \\ \hline 63 \end{array}$$

Nor did people divide. They subtracted. Dividing whole numbers is a short way of subtracting. If we want to know how many times 9 goes into 36, we write the problem like this: $9 \,\underline{|\;36}$
$\qquad 4$

That tells us that there are four 9's in 36. But we can also find that out by subtracting:

$$\begin{array}{r} 36 \\ -9 \\ \hline 27 \end{array} \qquad \begin{array}{r} 27 \\ -9 \\ \hline 18 \end{array} \qquad \begin{array}{r} 18 \\ -9 \\ \hline 9 \end{array} \qquad \begin{array}{r} 9 \\ -9 \\ \hline 0 \end{array}$$

Subtracting, we find there are four 9's in 36. We must take 9 away four times to get zero.

This is what people did with the abacus.

Index

ABOUT THE AUTHOR OF THIS BOOK

Patricia Lauber, formerly editor in chief of a science magazine for young people, is the author of many science books. Among them are *All About the Ice Age* and *All About the Planets.* Her Easy-to-Read stories for Random House include *Adventure at Black Rock Cave* and *Champ, Gallant Collie.* A graduate of Wellesley College, she lives in New York City.

ABOUT THE ILLUSTRATOR OF THIS BOOK

Mircea Vasiliu has illustrated many books for adults and young people, including his own *Everything Is Somewhere.* His autobiography, *The Pleasure Is Mine,* tells of his career as a Rumanian diplomat before becoming a United States citizen. He and his wife live in Riverdale, N.Y.

THE RANDOM HOUSE GATEWAY SCIENCE LIBRARY

Physical Science and Mathematics

Your Wonderful World of Science by Mae and Ira Freeman
Simple Machines and How They Work by Elizabeth N. Sharp
The Story of the Atom by Mae and Ira Freeman
The Story of Electricity by Mae and Ira Freeman
The Story of Chemistry by Mae and Ira Freeman
The Story of Numbers by Patricia Lauber

Space and Astronomy

The Sun, the Moon, and the Stars by Mae and Ira Freeman
The Earth in Space by John and Cathleen Polgreen
The World of Rockets by Alexander L. Crosby
Satellites in Outer Space by Isaac Asimov

Earth and Weather

Rocks All Around Us by Anne Terry White
In the Days of the Dinosaurs by Roy Chapman Andrews
Danger! Icebergs Ahead! by Lynn and Gray Poole
Hurricanes, Tornadoes, and Blizzards by Kathryn Hitte

Life Science

Your Body and How It Works by Patricia Lauber
Mammals and How They Live by Robert M. McClung
The Friendly Dolphins by Patricia Lauber
The Surprising Kangaroos by Patricia Lauber
The Swift Deer by Robert M. McClung
The Story of Dogs by Patricia Lauber
The Mighty Bears by Robert M. McClung

IV
XC
LDM

9203 00 667951 01 8 (IC=2)
LAUBER, PATRICIA 06/28/85
THE STORY OF NUMBERS
(3) [1961 JUV PZ 10.L23 ST

Juv. PZ10.L23 St
The story of numbers
3 2551 00039544 6